McGRATH MATH

TEDDY BEAR, TEDDY BEAR,
SCHOOL DAY MATH

CHOOL BUS

Barbara Barbieri McGrath

Illustrated by Tim Nihoff

Charlesbridge

Teddy Bear, Teddy Bear,
school's begun.
Count the teddies.
Join the fun!

Teddy Bear, Teddy Bear,
sit up straight.

Count by twos.
Do you see eight?

Teddy Bear, Teddy Bear,
touch the floor.

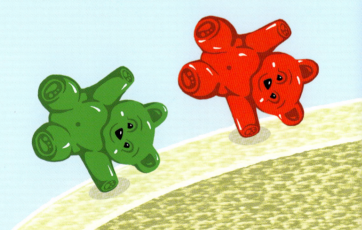

Which group of bears
has just four?

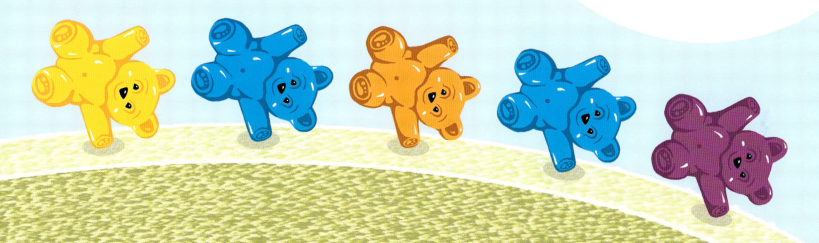

Teddy Bear, Teddy Bear,
pat your head.

Are there fewer yellow or red?

Teddy Bear, Teddy Bear,
turn around.

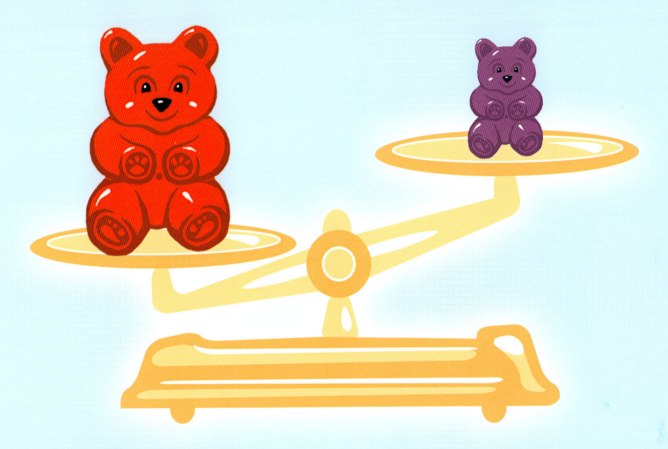

Which weighs more?
Good! Sit down!

Teddy Bear, Teddy Bear,
say your age.

How many bears
are on this page?

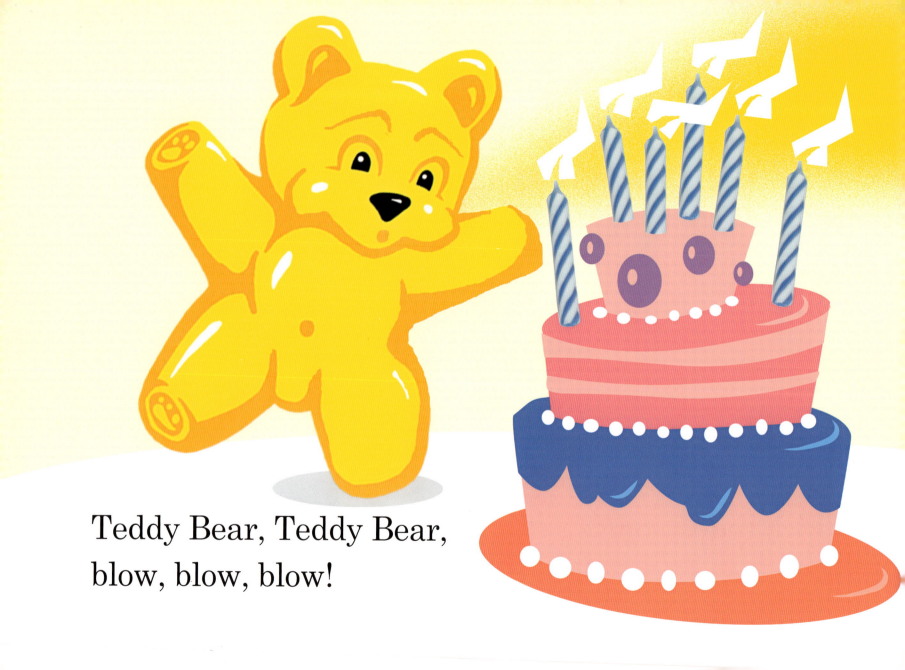

Teddy Bear, Teddy Bear,
blow, blow, blow!

Which teddy comes next
in this row?

Teddy Bear, Teddy Bear,
time to drive.
Which of these groups
has more than five?

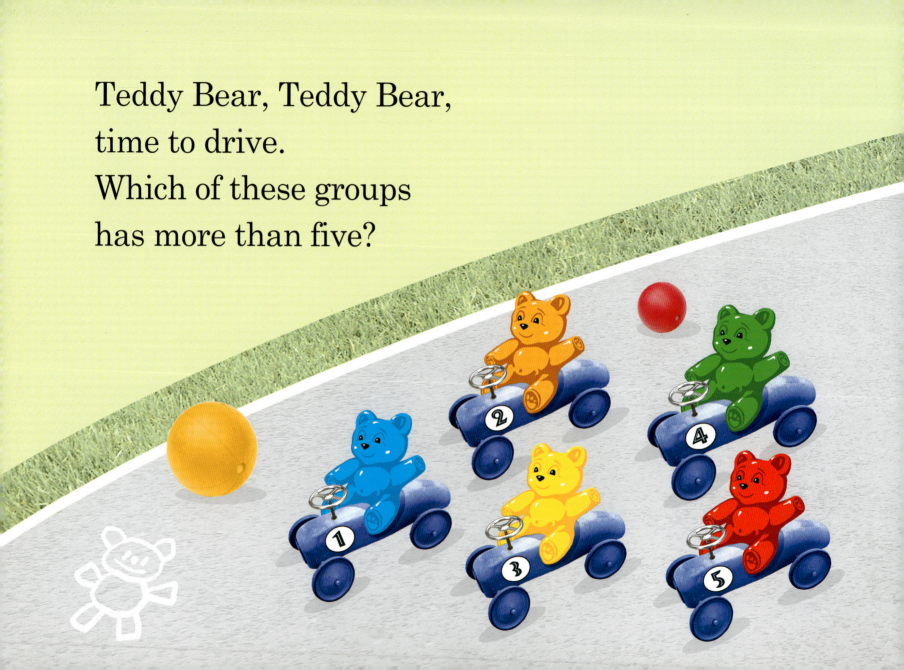

Teddy Bear, Teddy Bear,
fly, fly, flew.

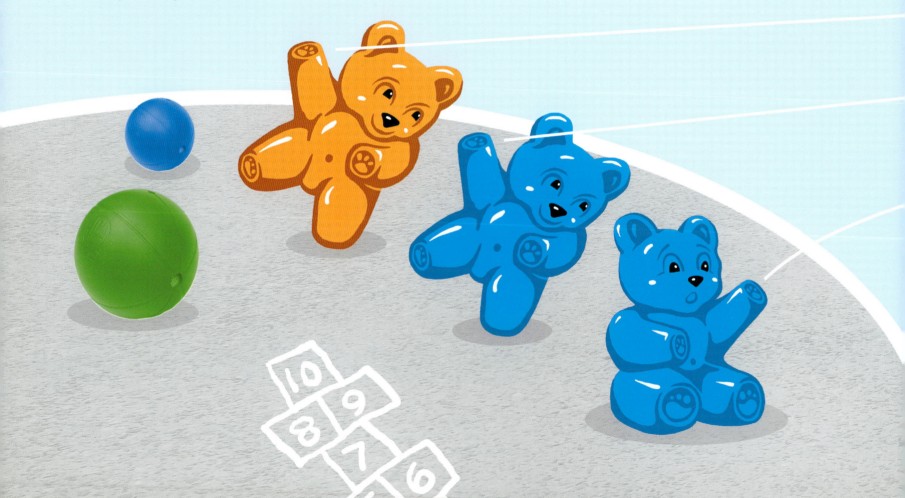

How many is one bear
plus these two?

Teddy Bear, Teddy Bear,
tie your shoe.

Are there fewer
green bears or blue?

Teddy Bear, Teddy Bear,
moo like a cow.

Which color bear
should line up now?

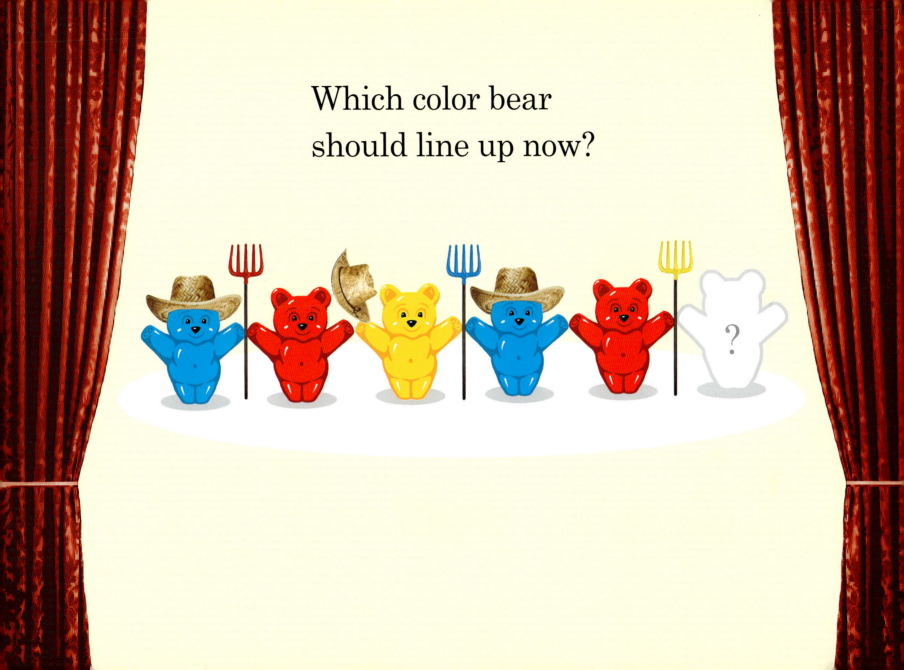

Teddy Bear, Teddy Bear,
clap and shout.

How many are left
when three sneak out?

Teddy Bear, Teddy Bear,
save a penny.
Count by fives
to see how many.

Teddy Bear, Teddy Bear,
a great big laugh.

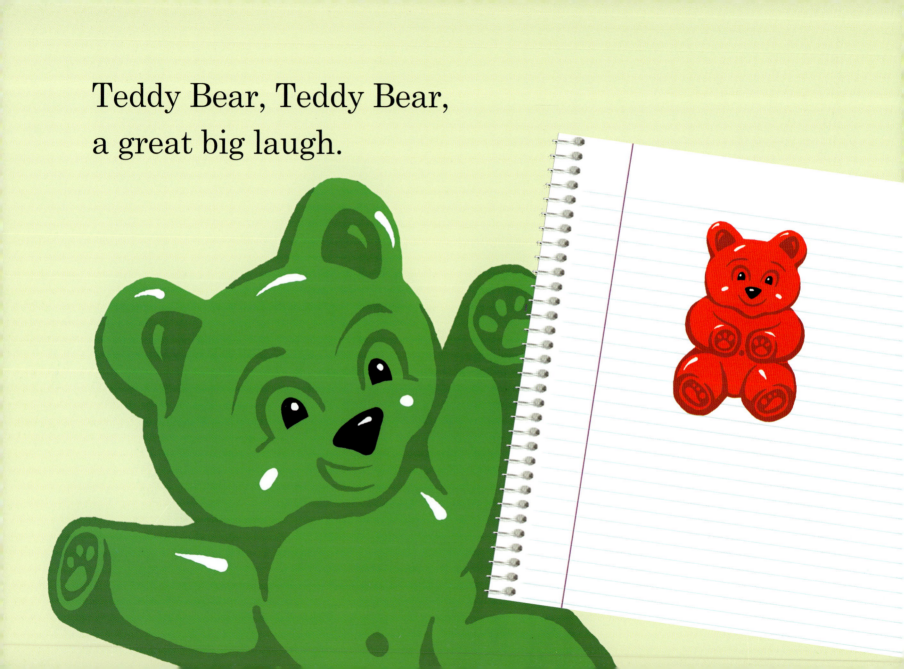

Which teddy bear
is a bear in half?

Teddy Bear, Teddy Bear,
jump or hop.
Teddy Bear, Teddy Bear,
this means STOP!

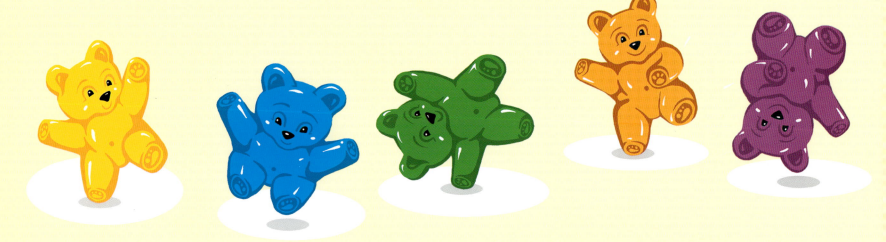

Text copyright © 2012 by Barbara Barbieri McGrath
Illustrations copyright © 2012 by Tim Nihoff

Published by Charlesbridge
85 Main Street
Watertown, MA 02472
(617) 926-0329
www.charlesbridge.com

Library of Congress Cataloging-in-Publication Data
McGrath, Barbara Barbieri, 1954–
    Teddy Bear, Teddy Bear, School Day Math / Barbara Barbieri McGrath;
Illustrated by Tim Nihoff.
        p. cm.
    ISBN 978-1-58089-420-3 (reinforced for library use)
    ISBN 978-1-58089-421-0 (softcover)
1. Counting—Juvenile literature. 2. Colors—Juvenile literature.
I. Nihoff, Tim. II. Title.
QA113.M39374 2012
513.2'11—dc23   2011025898

Printed in China
(hc) 10 9 8 7 6 5 4 3 2 1
(sc) 10 9 8 7 6 5 4 3 2 1

Illustrations hand drawn digitally and collaged with found objects
    in Adobe Photoshop
Display type set in Animated Gothic and text type set
    in Century Schoolbook
Color separations by KHL Chroma Graphics, Singapore
Printed and bound February 2012 by Jade Productions
    in Heyuan, Guangdong, China
Production supervision by Brian G. Walker
Designed by Whitney Leader-Picone

A bear hug to Branson.—B. B. M.

Debby Dargan (Art) + Ed Teska (Math) = Love
I cherish your sweet, playful, and mindful
teachings.—T. N.